– THE –
BRIGHTON LINE
A TRACTION HISTORY

Simon Jeffs

AMBERLEY PUBLISHING

Front Cover
Above: A painting of Brighton in the 1960s. (*Mike Turner*)

Below: On the moonlit night of 26 October 2007, all eight Class 460 Gatwick Express units pose at Stewarts Lane Depot. (*Courtesy of Southern*)

Back Cover
Above: 0-4-2 B1 Class No. 214 *Gladstone* was preserved in 1926 and is now part of the National Collection, residing at the National Railway Museum in York. (*Bruce Nathan*)

Below: 33004 prepares to leave the British Industrial Sand works at Holmethorpe, near Redhill, on 10 July 1986. (*Chris Wilson*)

First published 2013

Amberley Publishing
The Hill, Stroud
Gloucestershire, GL5 4EP

www.amberley-books.com

Copyright © Simon Jeffs, 2013

The right of Simon Jeffs to be identified as the Author of this work has been asserted in accordance with the Copyrights, Designs and Patents Act 1988.

ISBN 978 1 4456 1942 2
E-book ISBN 978-1-4456-1960-6

British Library Cataloguing in Publication Data.
A catalogue record for this book is available from the British Library.

Typeset in 9.5pt on 12pt Celeste.
Typesetting by Amberley Publishing.
Printed in the UK.

THE BRIGHTON LINE – A TRACTION HISTORY

The traction history of the Brighton Line, like so many other aspects of the Brighton story, is unique. As the line was built to serve what would now be called 'the leisure market', it was not overlaid on plateways or tramways serving collieries, mines or other industrial outlets. However, two short stretches of the moribund Croydon, Merstham & Godstone Iron Railway south of Coulsdon and much of the course of the Croydon Canal were incorporated into the route. The London & Croydon Railway adopted atmospheric traction between Norwood Junction and New Cross Gate and had plans to extend this to Epsom. However, the London, Brighton & South Coast Railway (LBSCR) ruled against this and the atmospheric system was dismantled and replaced by 'normal' steam-hauled trains.

Prior to 1846, steam locomotives were drawn from a pool of locomotives used by several companies and maintained at New Cross. Although Horley was briefly considered, the LBSCR Works were eventually established at Brighton. Locomotive building commenced in 1850 and continued until 1929. Between 1930 and 1942, locomotives, coaches and electric multiple units (EMUs) continued to be repaired at Brighton, but, under the aegis of the Southern Railway, new build transferred to Eastleigh and Ashford. However, by 1942 the Works were re-equipped and began to produce locomotives again – 104 of Bulleid's 'West Country' pacifics were assembled there. The last engine left the Works in March 1957, Class 4 Standard 2-6-4T No. 80154, and the run-down began. For a while, they were used to assemble motor cars but final closure and demolition came in 1969.

Steam was, of course, the major form of traction on the Brighton Line until 1909 when the line between London Bridge and Victoria was electrified using a 6,700 V AC overhead line system (OHLE) and a fleet of EMUs. Once the Southern Railway was formed in 1923, the now-familiar third rail 660 V DC system was adopted and progressively spread across the South London suburbs, replacing the 6,700 V AC system from 1928 and extending to Brighton by 1933. From this date, steam traction was confined to goods, excursions, boat trains and Oxted Line services on the Brighton. The Southern had planned to electrify its entire system east of the London-Southampton line but the Second World War and nationalisation put paid to that. By 1993, third rail electrification had reached its fullest extent to date and, since that time, nearly all passenger services on and connecting with the main Brighton line have been operated by EMUs or electric locos, with the exception of the London Bridge–Uckfield, Gatwick Airport –Redhill–Reading, Brighton–Ashford International and inter-regional services which are operated by diesel multiple units (DMUs) or diesel locomotives. In 2013, the all-third rail electric passenger railway presents a totally different railway image to the rest of the United Kingdom and, despite, irreverent references to it being a tramway rather than a 'proper' railway, the Southern Electric system continues to move vast quantities of passengers around the southern counties and London with great efficiency. To give an idea of this, Victoria was the second busiest station in the UK with over 73 million entries

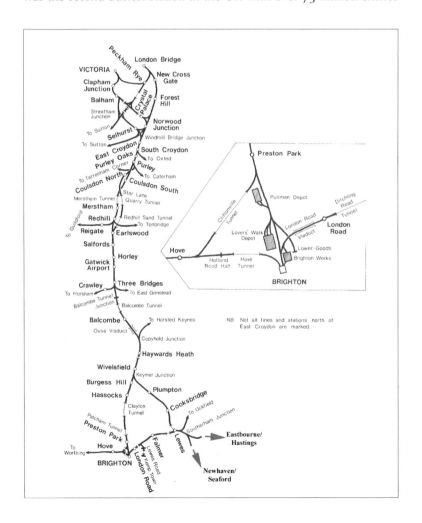

and exits during 2010–11, while East Croydon saw over 20 million, Brighton 14.5 million and Gatwick Airport 13 million in the same year. Such numbers demand a rapid transit system based on multiple units with fast turn-around at termini, high passenger capacity, rapid acceleration and low maintenance, to which the current fleet of Class 313, 319, 377, 442 and 455/6 units operated by Southern and First Capital Connect are ideally-suited.

The story of Brighton line traction is thus one of ever-increasing passenger traffic, relatively minimal and declining (from 1963) freight and technological innovation. The route is now considered to be at capacity and massive expenditure will be required to cope with increasing passenger numbers. While conversion to 25 kV OHLE has been considered, particularly after the annual few days of disruption due to snow and ice, it is likely that, unless 'HS3' is built between London and Brighton, the third rail EMU will reign supreme for many years yet.

This survey of Brighton line traction covers the period 1841–September 2013. As steam traction has been extensively covered in numerous publications, and electric services commenced in 1909, I will concentrate on non-steam traction, particularly the third rail EMUs for which the Brighton Line was (and still is) renowned. The book concludes with a brief survey of preserved traction that has operated on the Brighton, focusing on operational steam, diesel and electric locomotives and multiple units in the south of England.

A painting of Brighton in the 1960s. (*Mike Turner*)

BRIGHTON LINE STEAM LOCOMOTIVES

1841–1922 (LBR AND LBSCR)

Initially, the London & Brighton Railway (LBR) and, thereafter, the LBSCR, did not build its own locos, but obtained them from established manufacturers (see below). It was not until the appointment of John Chester Craven as Locomotive Superintendent in 1847 that the Works at Brighton were established and loco building started in Sussex. Craven retired in 1869, to be followed by William Stroudley (1870–1889), Robert John Billinton (1890–1904), D. Earle Marsh (1905–1911) and, finally, Lawson Billinton (son of Robert) until 1922 when the LBSCR was subsumed into the Southern Railway. Each Locomotive Superintendent was responsible for the design and manufacture of locomotives from humble shunting engines through to those designed for the fastest expresses. A feature of loco development throughout this period was the increasing weight and speed of both goods and passenger trains. Thus, a 'Jenny Lind' of 1847 would not be suitable for the heavy Pullman trains of the 1920s. Equally, advances in railway technology would be applied with each successive build. Space precludes a description of all the locos used on the LBR and LBSCR, but a bibliography is provided where further information can be obtained.

One of the famous 'Jenny Lind' 2-2-2 locomotives, designed by David Joy for the LBSCR and built by E. B. Wilson & Company in 1847. Jenny Lind was a celebrated Swedish opera singer of the time, and 'Jenny Linds' became the class name for this design. (*Ian Allan Ltd.*)

John Craven is pictured, with his family, in front of 2-4-0T 'Crystal Palace' tank engine No. 12 at Brighton in May 1858. Craven presided over the LBSCR during its period of expansion and, as each new line was opened, he designed a different class of locomotive to work it. On his retirement in 1869, the company owned 233 engines divided into seventy-two different classes! (*Paul Edwards Collection*)

The Brighton made prolific use of tank engines for passenger services as the journey from London to the Sussex coast did not require large supplies of coal and water. Craven's successor, William Stroudley, was responsible for three major classes of tank engines. The Class A1 0-6-0T Terriers for suburban passenger services, the 0-4-2T 'maids of all work, Class D1 and the Class E1, which were principally used as goods engines. One E1 has been preserved, B110. Several of the small, light Terrier locos were retained to work weight-restricted lines such as the Kent & East Sussex Railway, the Hayling Island branch and Newhaven West breakwater and the final example was not withdrawn from BR service until August 1963. Ten have been preserved, the doyen of which was No. 55, *Stepney*, which effectively started the standard gauge passenger heritage railway industry when she entered service on the Bluebell Railway in 1960. *Stepney* is seen here with the 4-4-2T LSWR Radial Tank No. 0415 on the Bluebell Railway. (*Mike Esau*)

For heavy goods and the most important passenger trains, tender engines were still favoured. For goods, the Class C and C1 0-6-0 locos were provided while Stroudley's first foray into express passenger engines was a 2-2-2 'single', No. 151 *Grosvenor*, introduced in 1874. Twenty-five locos of the G Class, derived from *Grosvenor*, were used on the principal LBSCR expresses from 1878. No. 344 *Hurstmonceux* is pictured. (*John Minnis collection*)

Next, Stroudley developed tender versions of the D1 tanks, in the shape of the Class D2 and D3 locos with a 0-4-2 wheel arrangement. In 1882, the first of the famous B1 Gladstone class emerged from Brighton works, followed by a further thirty-five locos. The doyen of the Class, No. 214 *Gladstone* himself, was the first railway engine to be preserved by a group of Railway Enthusiasts from the Stephenson Locomotive Society in December 1926. *Gladstone* now resides at the National Railway Museum in York, where it is seen in Stroudley's 'Improved Engine Green' livery. (*NRM*)

Stroudley was succeeded by Robert John Billinton. One of his major contributions to the LBSCR loco fleet were the 0-6-2T Radial Tank engines of Classes E3, E4, E5 and E6. The Radials covered all duties from shunting to fast passenger services well into the BR era. Class E4, No. 473 *Birch Grove*, has been preserved and is seen at Sheffield Park on the Bluebell Railway on 7 August 2011. (*Simon Jeffs*)

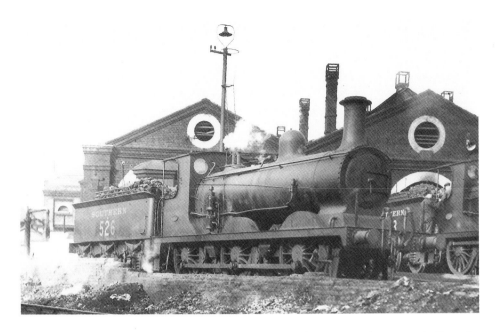

R. J. Billinton was also responsible for the C2 0-6-0 goods engines. These were built at the Vulcan Foundry in Newton-le-Willows, as Brighton was fully engaged churning out radial tanks. Vulcan Class C2X (a conversion of Class C2 by Marsh with a C3 boiler) loco No. 526 is seen at Brighton depot on 24 October 1934. (*H. C. Casserley*)

In 1895, Billinton's express passenger B2 Class appeared. This introduced the 4-4-0 wheel arrangement to the Brighton, but they were poor riders – their nickname of 'Grasshoppers' says it all – and something better was needed. This arrived in the shape of the fast, elegant B4 Class, many of which were built by Sharp, Stewart & Co. of Glasgow, with the inevitable moniker of 'Scotchmen'. B4 No. 68 runs into Haywards Heath with the 5.12 p.m. Hastings to Victoria service on the evening of the 19 July 1930. (*H. C. Casserley*)

Billinton was succeeded by D. Earle Marsh in 1905. Marsh wasted no time in bringing a 'huge express 4-4-2 express engine ... which was a copy of those on the Great Northern Railway' (Dendy Marshall) into service to work heavy expresses, especially the Southern Belle and Newhaven boat trains. Five emerged in 1905/6 (Class H1) and a further, superheated batch of six (Class H2) in 1911/12. H2 Class No. 32426 St Albans Head leaves London Bridge in the 1950s with a Brighton via Oxted train. (*Brian Morrison*)

H1 Class No. 38 passes South Croydon *c.* 1919 with a Brighton–Victoria train composed of Marsh 'Balloon' stock. (*Michael Baker Collection*)

Marsh also produced batches of I1, I2 and I4 4-4-2T locos for suburban work, but perfection was achieved by a version with 6 ft 7½ in. diameter wheels and, crucially, superheating – the I3 Class – emerging in 1907. During trials on the Sunny South Express in November 1909, I3 No. 23 (with no water scoop) never once needed to stop for water during the 77.2 miles non-stop run between Willesden and Rugby with a 250 ton train at an average speed of 53mph and the entire run from Rugby to Brighton and back was accomplished with 3¼ tons of coal. The LNWR was impressed, and superheating rapidly became essential for everything except shunting locos. I3 Class 2078 is seen poking out of the locomotive shed at New Cross Gate in 1927. (*H.C. Casserley*)

In 1910, Marsh produced a further large tank engine, this time with a 4-6-2 wheel arrangement, allowing a larger boiler to be fitted. J Class No. 325, *Abergavenny*, was employed, to great success with its post-Marsh sister No. 326 *Bessborough*, on the heaviest Pullman trains. *Abergavenny* poses for her official photograph. (*John Minnis Collection*)

Marsh was replaced by Lawson Billinton in 1911. Much of his period in office was taken up by the First World War and, subsequently, he produced few designs. After producing his E2 locos as replacements for the E1 Class 0-6-0T tanks, a fast, heavy goods engine was required. This was met by the K Class 2-6-0 locos from September 1913. Here is K Class 32344 doing the job it was built for, hauling a freight train through Redhill in the 1950s. (*Brian Morrison*)

Lawson is really remembered for the last, most spectacular LBSCR tank engines, the massive Class L 4-6-4T Baltic tanks. Two, 327 and 328, were produced during the War with another five, 329–333, emerging from Brighton after hostilities ceased. The very last was 333, *Remembrance*, which brought the curtain down on the LBSCR's long and fascinating steam locomotive history. Loco 331 pauses at East Croydon on 18 December 1926. (*H. C. Casserley*)

1923–1947 (SOUTHERN RAILWAY)

The first Chief Mechanical and Electrical Engineer of the new Southern Railway (SR) from 1923 was R. E. L. Maunsell from the South Eastern & Chatham Railway. The SR inherited a fleet of 2,281 steam locos from 108 classes. The LBSCR bequeathed its Radial tanks, the C2 and K Class goods locos and its fleet of express locos – the big I3, J and L Class tanks and the Marsh Atlantics. It soon became apparent that Brighton designs would not be perpetuated and although Brighton Works was tasked with the production of some of the 2-6-4T River Class passenger tanks, U Class 2-6-0 mixed traffic engines and the Z Class 0-8-0T goods tanks until 1929, thereafter loco building ceased and was transferred to Eastleigh and Ashford. Express loco needs on the Southern were met by Maunsell's 4-6-0 *King Arthur* and *Lord Nelson* and the 4-4-0 'Schools' designs. A batch of King Arthurs with six-wheel tenders saw out the last few years with the large tanks before electrification of the Brighton mainline, while a few Schools locos were used on Eastbourne and Ore services until that line joined the Southern Electric in 1935. With electrification of the Mid-Sussex line through Horsham to Portsmouth in 1938 and the total conversion of the London suburban network, steam was only required for secondary services, freight, boat trains and inter-regional excursion traffic on the LBSCR from 1938. Freight needs were met by the SECR 2-6-0 Mogul designs of Classes N, N1, U and U1,

The Southern Railway era. In March 1926, the last fourteen of Maunsell's N15 Class 4-6-0 King Arthur locos reached the Brighton line. No. 803, *Sir Harry le Fise Lake*, leaves Brighton with the 5.05 p.m. to Victoria on 30 April 1932. (*H. C. Casserley*)

the Class S15 4-6-0s, the 2-6-4T Class W and 0-8-0T Class Z tanks and, finally, the 0-6-0 Class Q.

Maunsell was succeeded by Oliver Bulleid in 1937. Initially, Bulleid's thinking was directed towards a replacement for the Lord Nelson express locos which duly arrived in the shape of the first 4-6-2 Merchant Navy Class in March 1941. Bulleid was a great innovator and packed many of his cherished ideas into this new loco – high-pressure boilers, thermic siphons, all-welded steel firebox, enclosed Walschaerts gear in an oil bath to provide continuous lubrication, streamlining – and even a new numbering system; the loco was 21C1, *Channel Packet*. Eventually, thirty were built, followed by 110 Light Pacific locos with a lower axle weight of 19 tons – the West Country Class. For freight, a fleet of the curious, but powerful, Q1 Class 0-6-0s were produced. Finally, to replace the elderly M7 0-4-4T engines, Bulleid came up with the double-ended 0-6-6-0T Leader Class loco, with a central firing position. Unfortunately, this revolutionary concept failed and the Leaders never entered service.

But the Big Tank policy was not yet finished. Ten K Class 2-6-4T 'River' locos entered work on the Brighton from the summer of 1925. A795 is seen at Coulsdon North on 28 May 1927. (*H. C. Casserley*)

The dour suburban station of Honor Oak Park is enlivened by the passage of Class V Schools 4-4-0 30930 *Radley* on an empty coaching stock (ECS) train in 1962. *Radley* and several other members of the class were stationed at Brighton at the time and became associated with Oxted Line services. (*A. J. Wills © Southern Railway Net*)

Maunsell's 2-6-0 Mogul locos of Classes N, N1, U and U1 stationed at Redhill, Brighton, Norwood Junction and Three Bridges depots took over a lot of the goods workings on the ex-LBSCR lines. Here, N Class 31812 trundles past Tinsley Green on 4 June 1946. (*H. C. Casserley*)

The three-cylinder version of the U Class moguls, the U1s, were often used on passenger services, particularly inter-regionals. Here, Class U1 2-6-0 No. 31900 is seen at Redhill with the Birkenhead train. (*Brian Morrison*)

Maunsell's last design was the Class Q 0-6-0 goods engine. 30537 stands outside Three Bridges shed in June 1962. (*Gordon Gravett*)

A 'Spam Can' at Brighton shed. 'Air-smoothed' Bulleid Light Pacific loco 34092 *City of Wells* awaits its next duty in June 1957 with E3 0-6-2T Radial Tank 32165 on the right. The Pacific has been preserved and is currently based on the Keighley & Worth Valley Railway, a long way from home, in Yorkshire. (*A. J. Wills © Southern Photo Net*)

As many of the older goods engines were withdrawn from service, a number of the newer Q1 Class o-6-os were moved to Three Bridges between 1962 and 1964 until the Class 33 diesels finally took over. 33018 stands on one of the turntable tracks in September 1963. (*Gordon Gravett*)

The unique 'Leader' loco. The photo shows partially-completed 36003 at Brighton Works awaiting scrapping on 20 May 1951 (*W. M. J. Jackson/courtesy Brian W. Jackson*)

1948–1967 (BRITISH RAILWAYS, SOUTHERN REGION)

With the abandonment of Bulleid's Leader project, British Railways Southern Region urgently needed some new tank engines. This was met by the construction of forty-one 2-6-4T locos to the design of the ex-LMSR engineer, Thomas Fairburn, at Brighton between 1950–51. Many operated on the Oxted and Wealden lines until replaced by an updated design from R. A. Riddles, the Class 4 Standard 2-6-4T tank. 130 of these were produced at Brighton, including 80154, the last loco to be built at the Works, which emerged on 20 March 1957. During the last two decades of steam, many of the old Southern and LBSCR designs were replaced by designs from elsewhere within British Railways. Tank engines from the London Midland Region became particularly prevalent on secondary services and freight. In June 1965, Redhill depot closed to steam. Although the occasional special still worked along the Brighton line until June 1967, regular steam services were over on the Brighton.

Fairburn Class 4MT No. 42093 is under assembly at Brighton Works on 8 May 1951 (*A. J. Wills* © *Southern Railway Net*)

Standard Class 4 2-6-4T No. 80144 simmers under the overall canopy of Platform 6 at Three Bridges with the 5.27 p.m. from East Grinstead in April 1965. These locos, along with the ex-LSWR M7 and ex-SECR H Class tanks, operated on the secondary Wealden and Oxted lines until the arrival of diesel electric multiple units from 1963. (*Gordon Gravett*)

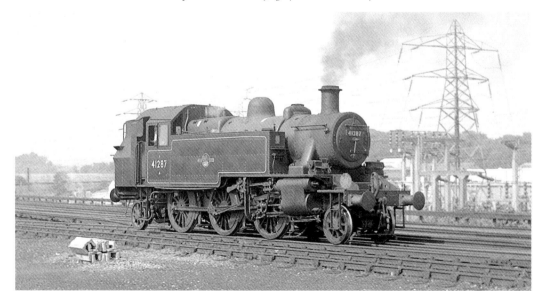

Although Three Bridges engine shed officially closed in January 1964, it was still used to service engines working into Horsham from Guildford. Most of these were Class 2 Ivatt 2-6-2T tanks, from a batch of thirty built at Crewe and allocated from new in 1951 to all three divisions of the Southern. Here, 41287 is seen backing into the shed yard in August 1964. (*Gordon Gravett*)

Ex-LSWR M7 and ex-SE&CR H 0-4-4Ts were the mainstay of the Three Bridges–East Grinstead line pull-push services during the 1950s and 1960s. M7 30133, allocated to Tunbridge Wells West, receives attention under the sheer legs at Three Bridges in September 1963. (*Gordon Gravett*)

Photos of Brighton line traction in the 1950s and 1960s tend to give the impression that everything was steam-hauled! However, a procession of excursion and holiday trains did head to and from the coast on Summer Saturdays and Bank Holidays. Here, an unidentified Black 5 4-6-0 passes the 'old' Gatwick Airport station on August Bank Holiday Monday in 1964. (*Gordon Gravett*)

And how on earth did that get here? A Jubilee Class 4-6-0, loco 45595 *Southern Rhodesia,* at Brighton waits to take a train back to Manchester. (*W. M. J. Jackson/courtesy Brian W. Jackson*)

Finally, a tribute to the men of steam. Driver George Laycock leans from the cab of Standard Class 4 2-6-4T No. 80019 on 20 June 1952. (*Ted Janes Collection*)

DIESEL AND ELECTRIC LOCOMOTIVES, 1937-2013

R. E. L. Maunsell undertook a number of experimental non-steam projects during his time in office. First was a 50 hp Drewry four-wheel railcar that was sold in 1934 but, in 1937, three 0-6-0 diesel shunters entered service. In 1937, Alfred Raworth's electrical design team started work on the design of an electric freight loco which evolved into a 1500 hp Co-Co mixed-traffic loco. Three were ordered, the first, CC1, emerging from Eastleigh in 1941. This was designed to work both on the 750V DC third rail and from a simple overhead wire, the latter to be employed in sidings and marshalling yards where a third rail would be a hazard. A flywheel system (or 'booster') allowed the loco to travel across short gaps in the third rail. CC1 proved highly efficient and was followed by two more locos, CC2 in 1943 and CC3/20003 in 1949. Plans were drawn up by the Southern in 1944 for the complete electrification of all lines east of the Basingstoke–Southampton axis, with steam locos replaced by a fleet of diesel shunting locomotive and fifty electric locos, similar to CC1. Austerity and the formation of British Railways put paid to this radical plan, but the unique nature of the Southern ensured that, well into the British Railways era, it retained an individualistic non-steam traction policy.

First diesels on the Southern. Nos. 1–3 (later 15201–3) were mechanically-similar to the later Class 08 units, with a 350 hp English Electric power unit. No. 3 is seen being overhauled at Brighton Works on 1 October 1949. This design was later improved and expanded by Bulleid, with 15211–36 entering service from 1949. (*A. J. Wills* © *Southern Railway Net*)

Bulleid was responsible for two diesel locomotive prototypes. The first, 11001, was a 500 hp diesel mechanical 0-6-0 designed for both shunting and trip working, but proved unsuitable for either. (*Arthur Tayler*)

The second was an express passenger loco to be used on a high-speed Waterloo–Plymouth service. Three were ordered, 10201–3, the last being built at Brighton in 1954. They spent most of their time operating out of Waterloo on West of England services before transfer to the London Midland region. British Railways' first express passenger diesel loco, the English Electric Type 4 (D200–D399 – later Class 40), was very closely based on them. 10203 is seen at Crowborough on its first trial run from Brighton Works in March 1954. (*Arthur Tayler*)

The three Raworth/Bulleid electric locos were nicknamed 'Boosters' or, later, 'Hornbys'. CC1/2 were renumbered 20001/2 in 1949 and later received BR Blue livery with full yellow ends. 20001 is seen on its final duty, the Sussex Venturer railtour, at a very foggy Lewes on 4 January 1969. (*Clinton Shaw*)

The Hornbys did look rather splendid in their lined-out BR Green livery. Prior to the fitting of a head code box, 20002 is seen fresh from overhaul at Eastleigh Works in 1964. The locos were withdrawn in 1968/9 without renumbering as Class 70. (*Clinton Shaw*)

Loco 20003 was different in appearance to the other two, having a flat front akin to the all-steel 4 Sub units of the period. A favourite duty for all three Hornbys was the Newhaven Boat train. 20003 is seen at Victoria on 15 April 1949, the first time this service was hauled by an electric loco. (*Arthur Tayler*)

The next electric locos on the Southern Region were the British Railways-designed Class HA (later Class 71) Bo-Bos. Their design was influenced by contemporary Swiss and French railway practice and, like the Hornbys, they carried a booster unit to get through gaps in the third rail and pantographs for yard work. Relatively rare on the Brighton, they did work some van and goods trains and, occasionally, the Newhaven Boat Train with a steam loco in tow to provide steam heating! A goods train is seen at Redhill with E5005 in charge. (*A. J. Wills © Southern Railway Net*)

Booster technology and tramline overhead wires were all very well but, as long ago as 1944, the Southern had started design work on an electric locomotive with an auxiliary power unit to operate away from conductor rails or wires. Eventually, six prototype 1600hp electric/600hp diesel Bo-Bo 'Electro-Diesels' were built with the first, E6001, emerging from Eastleigh in February 1962. E6001 is seen at South Croydon with a parcels/mail train in 1976. (*Michael Baker*)

On introduction, the first six electro-diesels (E6001-6) bore a green livery with white band above the solebar, reproduced on preserved loco E6003 (named *Sir Herbert Walker*), seen here on the Mid-Hants Railway on 20 June 1993. (*Adrian Willats*)

Later classified Class 73, due to their light weight and dual-power, the electro-diesels could operate anywhere on the Southern system. 73202 *Royal Observer Corps* & 73201 *Broadlands* 'top and tail' the Royal Train near Smitham on 9 June 1995, travelling from Windsor & Eton Riverside to Tattenham Corner for the Epsom Derby. (*Brian Morrison*)

The Class 73s' glory days were on the Gatwick Express passenger service between 1984 and 2005. At Gatwick Airport on 6 August 1985, 73127 (right) in 'large logo' BR Blue livery waits to return on the 12:20 service to Victoria while an InterCity-liveried example has just arrived on the left. (*Don Benn*)

Many of the Class 73 locos remain in service today. Two of them, 73119 *Borough of Eastleigh* and 73207, are seen at Sheffield Park on the Bluebell Railway after arriving on the Blue Belle railtour, on 23 March 2013 the first through service from Victoria since the Bluebell was extended to East Grinstead. (*Simon Jeffs*)

In 1952, the Southern Region was considering dieselisation of certain secondary lines and loco 10800 was sent to Brighton for tests. Built by the North British Locomotive Company and fitted with a Paxman 16 RPHXL engine that was not entirely suitable for rail traction, it failed frequently and became known as the 'Wonder' engine, as in 'I wonder if it will go today?' 10800 is seen at Brighton on 3 September 1952 after working the 3.52 p.m. from Victoria via Eridge. (*A. J. Wills © Southern Railway Net*)

To cover a shortage of electrically-heated carriage stock on the Kent Coast lines, sixteen boiler-fitted Sulzer Type 2 diesels (later Class 24), Nos D5000-14/17, were borrowed from the London Midland region and based at Hither Green between 1959 and 1962. They often ended up hauling portions of the Birkenhead–Margate/Hastings train from Redhill, where an unidentified member of the class is seen in June 1960. Q1 Class 0-6-0 steam loco 33003 simmers in the background. (*A. J. Wills © Southern Railway Net*)

The Southern Region's custom-designed Class 3 Loco was the 'Crompton', later Class 33. Built by the Birmingham Railway & Carriage Works, with a 1550 bhp Sulzer engine and Crompton Parkinson transmission equipment, the Cromptons had electrical train heating, a Southern-type route indicator between the cab windows and, with a weight of around 74 tons, could go nearly anywhere. Ninety-eight were built, and entered service from January 1960. By 1963, they were working passenger services on the Oxted and Wealden lines and some turns between Reading and Redhill. With the electro-diesels, they also took over nearly all freight working and inter-regionals from the same period, displacing many steam locos. Eventually, many of their passenger duties were displaced by DEMUs and further electrification and, with declining freight traffic, the last examples were withdrawn in February 2001. Twenty-six examples are preserved. Trundling an unfitted freight past the Greyhound pub between Three Bridges and Gatwick Airport, D6515 heads north in August 1964. (*Gordon Gravett*)

Hurtling through Purley, 6525 heads for the London Midland region with an excursion on 16 July 1972. (*Bryan Rayner*)

Now reclassified as Class 33/0, 33004 prepares to leave the British Industrial Sand works at Holmethorpe, near Redhill, on 10 July 1986. (*Chris Wilson*)

For a period between the withdrawal of the Class 33 fleet and the introduction of the GM-EMD Class 66 locos, many of the aggregates trains on the Brighton line were hauled by the powerful (3250 bhp) Electroputere/BREL Class 56 locos. 56060 approaches Redhill on Crawley New Yard to Merehead empties on 8th June 1997. (*Alex Dasi-Sutton*)

Once, nearly every Southern Railway freight yard, depot or works had its shunting locomotives. Initially steam, they were replaced by a variety of 0-6-0 diesels equipped with 350 bhp English Electric or 204 bhp Gardner engines. The Bulleid designs of the larger engines became Class 12, while the BR examples became Class 08. A subset of the latter, re-geared for a top speed of 27 ½ mph and fitted with air brakes, became Class 09. Amazingly, only ONE shunter remains in active use on the Brighton line. 09026, *Cedric Wares*, is seen at Brighton Lovers Walk depot on 1 May 2011. (*Colin Duff*)

The only other loco based on the Brighton line is the electro-diesel 73202 Dave Berry, operated by Gatwick Express and kept at Stewarts Lane. It is seen at Brighton on 1 May 2011. (*Colin Duff*)

In 1979, British Rail reintroduced daily inter-regional services between Brighton and the North West hauled by Brush Type 4 locos fitted with electric train heating (Class 47/4 or 47/8). Class 47/4 No. 47507 passes Coulsdon North signalbox on 26 January 1984, hauling the 07:38 cross-country service from Wolverhampton to Brighton. (*Brian Morrison*)

Most freight and many permanent way services on the Brighton line are now hauled by the ubiquitous Canadian-built General Motors Electro Motive Division (GM-EMD – now owned by Caterpillar) JT42CWR Co-Co locomotives, known as Class 66 in the UK. Here 66845 heads the 07:00 Daventry–Dollands Moor intermodal through Redhill on 17 July 2012 (*Alex Dasi-Sutton*). Some freight remains in the hands of the earlier GM-EMD Class 59 diesels while Class 73 electro-diesels assist with permanent way trains.

Network Rail trains are operated by a variety of Class 31, 37, 67 or 73 locos, while the occasional excursion or railtour is usually Class 47- or 67-hauled. The 30 Class 67 Bo-Bo locos were built by Alstom in Valencia, Spain, with EMD equipment, between 1999 and 2000. 67025 is seen at Redhill on 3 March 2006 with a Network Rail working. (*Arthur Tayler*)

Just about any type of diesel locomotive could turn-up on an inter-regional freight or passenger excursion, but they don't come much rarer than this Type 1 North British D84xx loco on an excursion from the Eastern Region at New Cross Gate on 21 June 1959. (*J. J. Smith*)

Not the best image, but it does show that the Class 27 locos were not confined to Scotland, as some were shedded at Cricklewood in the 1960s and worked a daily freight to Brighton. D5385 is seen at East Croydon in July 1967. (*Simon Jeffs*)

ELECTRIC AND DIESEL MULTIPLE UNITS, 1909–2013

The first EMUs on the LBSCR were the 6700 V AC OHLE SL stock of 1909 for the South London Line, followed by the CP and CW fleets for the extensions to Crystal Palace and Coulsdon/Sutton, respectively. After 1928, the OHLE stock was converted to various species of third rail 660V DC units, along with many types of three-car suburban units (and two-car trailer units) provided by the Southern Railway, as the third rail system expanded. In 1939, a ten-year plan was prepared to cover modernisation and reformation of the suburban units, using a mixture of new build, re-bodying (on pre-war underframes) and augmentation with an extra vehicle to provide the familiar '4 Sub' fleet. Production of 4 Sub units was continued by British Railways, eventually ceasing in 1951. By now, the old, augmented stock was getting a bit rickety and was progressively replaced by a fleet of two- and four-car EPB units between 1951–7. Again, some of these used pre-war underframes and augmentation all-steal trailers. The Southern has always been very good at recycling! The post-war 4 Sub fleet (latterly Class 405) was phased out by 1983. Many of the EPB fleet (now Classes 415 and 416) were extensively refurbished in the mid-1980s and lasted until 1995. The third generation of suburban stock was represented by the 1983 Class 455 units, the first units on the Brighton with sliding doors. Currently, these units share suburban duties with the 2-car Class 456 units (until 2014) and the Class 377 Electrostars.

For the Brighton mainline electrification of 1932–3, a fleet of 4 Lav units were provided for semi-fast and stopping services, while express duties were covered by the six-car 6 Cor (6 Pul from 1935) units, which incorporated a Pullman car for refreshments; the three six-car 6 Cor (6 Cit from 1935) units, with extra First Class accommodation for peak hour workings and the famous trio of Brighton Belle five-car 5 Pul (5 Bel from 1935) units. As electrification reached Eastbourne and Hastings and Portsmouth *via* Horsham and Chichester, furtherfleets of six-car 6 Pan, four-car 4 Cor and 4 Buf and two-car 2 Bil units entered service. The last of the pre-war Southern Railway mainline designs were represented by the 1938 Bulleid development of the 2 Bils, the 2 Hal units. The first post-Maunsell era express units were a small batch of 4 Cep and 4 Bep (with buffet car) four-car units that were based on the BR Mark I coach design with EP braking. However, squadron production of this design was intended for the Kent Coast Electrification projects and the Pul/Pan stock was actually succeeded by the '1963 Brighton Replacement Stock', the four-car 4 Cig and 4 Big fleet (later Class 421 and 422) from 1963, while four-car 4 Vep units swept away the Lav/Bil/Hal vehicles from 1968. By 1972, the only remnants of the Southern Railway mainline express fleet were the 5 Bel units, which sadly retired in May of that year, plus a few 4 Cors that clung on until October. Now the Ceps, Cigs and Veps had dominion.

Although the Cig/Big/Vep fleets (now Classes 421, 422 and 423) were extensively refurbished in the 1980s, all had been withdrawn by November 2005. A number of events hastened their demise, including the tragic rail crash at Clapham Junction on 12 December 1988 which exposed the structural weakness of slam-door stock and the re-opening of the Snow Hill tunnel between Blackfriars and Farringdon in 1988 accompanied by a fleet of eighty-six new dual-voltage, sliding-door, four-car EMUs (Class 319). This, coupled with expanding electrification, permitted a cascade of older stock to other parts of Network Southeast and the withdrawal of many of the Diesel Electric Multiple Units (DEMU). However, the major factor was probably that, following the privatisation of Britain's railways in 1994, it became more cost-effective to replace stock rather than modify it to generate additional revenue and meet new, more stringent, safety and disability access regulations. Thus, from 2001, the Class 4xx 'Slammers' were replaced by the 'Electrostar' Class 377 units, built by Bombardier at Derby and the Electro-Diesel hauled Gatwick Express trains were replaced by the distinctive eight-car Class 460 units built by Alstom. Thameslink services are covered by the aforementioned Class 319 units and a batch of Class 377/5 Electrostars.

Overcrowding on Brighton line peak services led to the refurbishment and transfer of the five-car Class 442 units from South West Trains to Southern from December 2008. These comfortable units now cover all Gatwick Express diagrams (some of which were extended to and from Brighton during the peaks), plus extra hourly services between Brighton and Victoria and a few peak London Bridge to Eastbourne workings. The last Class 460 was taken out of use in August 2012 to be reconfigured with Class 458 EMUs (which have identical electrical equipment) to create a new fleet of five-car Class 458/5 units from 2013 to be used by South West Trains.

Coastal services from Brighton have an EMU history all of their own. Stopping services along the Sussex coast to Worthing from 1933 were initially in the hands of twelve three-car ex-LSWR suburban units, but these were replaced early in 1935, by the 2 Nol units. The Nols survived until 1958, to be replaced by 2 Hap units. A few 4 Cor units also saw out their last days on Brighton–Seaford/Ore services. From 1982, a pair of Haps were permanently coupled to form the 4 Cap units, which lasted until 1995 and were succeeded by a variety of Class 4xx units, displaced from mainline duties, which in their turn were replaced by, miracle of miracles, brand new, air conditioned, three-car Class 377/3 Electrostar units! Of course, this couldn't last and the 377/3s went to London to be replaced by extensively-refurbished three-car Class 313/2 units. These are now the second oldest EMUs in BR service, dating from 1976. While suitable for a short trip, a journey from Brighton to Portsmouth in one of these units is something of an ordeal.

Turning to diesel units, one must first consider another unique Southern Region institution, the DEMU. A total of seventy-five of these were built between 1957–62 for services between London and Hastings (via Tonbridge) and unelectrified secondary lines in Hampshire, Berkshire, Sussex, Surrey and Kent. Basically, they were diesel versions of contemporary EMUs with the same EE507 traction motors and much other equipment shared with the EPB and Hap fleets but the prime mover was an English Electric 4SRKT diesel engine, developing 500 or 600 bhp. Three fleets were provided, six-car units of restricted width for Hastings duties (Classes 6S, 6L and 6B, later Class 203); three-and two-car units for use on secondary services in Hants and Berks and the Hastings–Ashford trains (initially 3H/2H, later Classes 205/204); and three-car 3D units (later Class 207) for East Sussex routes. The usual SR reformations and rebuilds occurred, the most notable of which was the formation of six 3-car 3R units in 1965, comprising two restricted-width 6S vehicles (including the motor coach) and a full-width (9 foot) driving trailer taken from a 2 EPB EMU of the 57xx series. These characterful units operated on the Tonbridge–Redhill–Reading route, where they rapidly earned the nickname of 'Tadpoles'! Electrification and line closures led to the shuffling around and withdrawal of the DEMU fleet, but the last examples survived on Uckfield trains until December 2004, forty-seven years after their introduction. The Tadpoles were replaced on Reading–Redhill–Tonbridge trains by Class 119 DMUs from the Western Region from 1979, while Network SouthEast introduced the 'Networker Turbos' of Classes 165 and 166 to the route, which they still operate today, although only between Gatwick Airport and Reading, Redhill–Tonbridge having been electrified in 1993.

Two other classes of DMU should be mentioned. The Brighton–Hastings–Ashford and Uckfield–London Bridge services are in the hands of a fleet of two- and four-car Class 171 Turbostar units, while the Class 47+ Mk II coaches operating the InterCity services between Brighton and the North were also replaced by 'Voyager' Class 220 DMUs from May 2001. However, these latter services were withdrawn in December 2008.

Eight three-car SL units were built in 1908-9 at the Metropolitan Amalgamated Railway & Carriage & Wagon Co.'s (MARCW) Saltley (Birmingham) works. Later, they were reformed as two-car units, with one SL driving motor paired with one CP-style driving trailer composite with two First Class compartments. (*Noodle Books collection*)

The SL units could not fit through Crystal Palace tunnel, so a new CP fleet of thirty-four three-car units was assembled by MARCW and the LBSCR's own works at Lancing. They were maintained at a new facility at Selhurst – the start of the enormous maintenance depot that is located there today. A CP unit is seen at Victoria. (*SEG Archives*)

For the Coulsdon and Wallington scheme, a third type of EMU was produced. Perhaps with eventual electrification of the main lines in mind, the trailers were similar to those of the CP stock but they were powered by short-framed motor luggage vans (MLV) instead of motored passenger cars. The majority of the trailers were built at Lancing and Eastleigh, but the MLVs were built by MARCW. A five-car rake, with the MLV in the centre, rests in the sidings at Coulsdon North. (*Noodle Books collection*)

The SL units were converted to third rail operation in 1928 and reclassified 2 SL. Renumbered 1801–8, two units enter London Bridge in 1954, the last year of their lives. (*David Brown collection*)

THIRD RAIL EMUs, SOUTHERN RAILWAY AND BRITISH RAILWAYS 1928–1965

A total of 466 three-car suburban units (never 3 Sub) were eventually provided, operating on the ex-LBSCR, SER and LSWR suburban lines. Operating singly off-peak, they were often combined with another unit, sandwiching a two-car trailer unit (converted from steam stock, as were many of the EMU bodies themselves) for peak services. When electrification was extended from Brighton to West Worthing in 1933, a small batch of ex-LSWR three-car suburban units was sent south to operate the stopping services for a while until the 2 Nol units arrived. One is seen arriving at West Worthing in 1933. (*David Brown collection*)

Augumented 4 Sub – 1: Unit 4507, one of a class of 17 (4501-17), formed using converted AC stock in 1956–7, is seen here at Forest Hill. (*A. J. Wills collection © Southernrailway.net*)

Augumented 4 Sub – 2: Unit 4319, from the back of twenty-five three-car units built new in 1925 for the Guildford via Epsom and Cobham electrification and seen here at East Croydon, was one of the units augumented with a Bulleid 1941-type steel-panelled (but with wood and canvas roof) trailer (second vehicle). (*A. J. Wills collection © Southernrailway.net*)

Orders for thirty new units were placed in 1939 and the first, 4101, emerged in October 1941. All accommodation was in (rather narrow) compartments, and the bodysides were built of sheeted steel with a distinctive, rounded profile. The cab front was similar to a 2 Hal. Their width and capacity soon earned them the nickname 'Shebas' from the Biblical passage concerning the Queen of Sheba arriving in Jerusalem with a 'very great train'! 4103 is seen at Clapham Junction in June 1967. (*SEG Archives*)

From unit 4111 onwards, all the new-build Subs had a steel roof and a flat front. Various permutations of interior design were deployed, until the 'Standard Unit' format was settled on in 1948. All Subs would now have three coaches with open saloons and one with compartments. 'Standard' Sub 4287 is seen at East Croydon in 1960 with a Coulsdon North train. (*A. J. Wills collection © Southernrailway.net*)

Subs did escape to the seaside on excursions. 4379 heads past Gatwick Airport old station towards Brighton on Bank Holiday Monday, August 1964.(*Gordon Gravett*)

Subs for the Oxted line? A curious, electrically-heated, high-capacity trailer unit, 900 (later, 701) set was formed in 1963 for use on peak-hour Oxted line services. This was formed of five ex-4 Sub vehicles sandwiched between the Motor Cars of ex-2 Bil unit 2006. The fourth vehicle was a nine-compartment coach from unit 4115, fitted out as a composite with First Class accommodation – the only 4 Sub vehicle ever to convey First Class passengers. 701 was withdrawn in May 1969. (*SEG Archives*)

Mainstay of the express fleet for the Brighton electrification were the twenty 6 Pul units, 2001–2020 (3001–3021 from 1937). These included a unique Composite Pullman Car, serving First and Second Class passengers, seen in the centre of unit 3013 on an Eastbourne service just south of Clapham Junction. (*SEG Archives*)

For the Eastbourne and Ore electrification of 1935, a similar fleet of 6 Pan units, in the number series 2021–2037 (later 3021–37), was provided. As the name suggests, a small pantry facility replaced the expensive Pullman cars. Unit 3024 passes Forest Hill signal box on a fast London Bridge–Brighton service. (*SEG Archives*)

The replacement for the popular Southern Belle steam-hauled Pullman train was provided by three five-car 5 Bel units, 2051–3 (later 3051–3), the first all-electric Pullman trains in the world. Starting as the Southern Belle in January 1933, it became the familiar Brighton Belle from June 1934. Surely the most famous train on the Brighton line, the 'Belles' were withdrawn on 30 April 1972. All fifteen cars were preserved, fourteen survive and a reborn Bel unit is currently being restored at Barrow Hill in Derbyshire by the 5Bel Trust. Unit 3051 passes Coulsdon North on 29 May 1968 on the 11:00 Victoria–Brighton service. (*John Scrace*)

Even the Belles had to fit British Rail's corporate blue-and-grey image. They never looked quite the same. 'Blue Belle' unit 3053 passes Thornton Heath on 8 August 1969. (*John Scrace*)

The First Class interior of refurbished Belle car *Doris* still retains its marquetry, Art Deco finishes, clock and comfortable seats, albeit reupholstered in InterCity charcoal and grey moquette. (*Simon Jeffs*)

In contrast, the refurbished Second Class cars looked rather archaic, with the same moquette used in the Veps contrasting with the fading woodwork. Car 90, the only one to be scrapped, is pictured on 28 April 1972, two days from withdrawal. (*Fred Matthews*)

Three additional 6 Pul units (2041–3, later 3041–3 and reclassified 6 Cit), with additional First Class seating, were provided for the peak business trains between Brighton, Worthing and London. Later, all three were re-classified as 6 Pul with the same First Class seating capacity as a 'normal' Pul. Unit 3041 is seen south of Balham with a Brighton Express. (*SEG Archives*)

Semi-fast and stopping services were in the hands of the thirty-three 4 Lav units, 1921–53 (later 2921–53). These appeared in 1932 and were the first non-suburban Southern Electric stock. They also initiated the Southern's obsession with lavatories – there are not four lavatories in these units, only two in one vehicle of a four-car unit. It paid to be in the right car on a long journey! Unit 2922 approaches South Croydon. (*SEG Archives*)

The 2 Bil units actually did have two lavatories, one in each coach of these two-car units. Designed for semi-fast and stopping services, 152 examples were built between 1935 and 1939, the last examples surviving until July 1971. One has been preserved by the National Railway Museum (NRM), 2090. 2142 is seen at Redhill on the Reigate shuttle in 1960. (*A.J. Wills collection © Southernrailway.net*)

The 2 Hal units had one lavatory per two-car unit. Seventy-five units (2601–2676) were built for the Eastern Section electrification to Maidstone and Gillingham in 1938/9, while 2677–92 were ordered as additional stock with no stated allocation. Displaced by the Hap/Cep stock in the 1958 Kent Coast elecrification, about thirty-five Hals were moved from the Eastern section to work Gatwick Airport services which were tied in to improved local services on the mid-Sussex line. Although superficially-similar to the Bils, they were notorious for their hard Third Class seating. 2615 arrives at East Croydon in 1970 with a Bognor Regis train. (*A. J. Wills collection © Southernrailway.net*)

To replace wartime losses, seven additional 2 Hal units (2693–99) emerged from Eastleigh in 1948 plus one more, 2700, in 1955. Of revised design, very similar to the new all-steel 4 Sub units, 2693–2699 became known as 'Tin Hals' and were often seen on Gatwick Airport workings after the new airport opened in May 1958. Blessed with a 2 ton-capacity luggage area, they were ideal for this traffic although their rough riding must have made a poor impression on airline passengers! Unit 2695 is seen at Three Bridges on 19 September 1970. (*John Scrace*)

And, yes, the 2 Nols had no lavatories! Their vehicles were formed of LSWR steam stock bodies mounted on new underframes and left Eastleigh between 1934 and 1936 to work a variety of services including Sussex coastal stoppers, thus commencing a tradition of these routes receiving old, basic stock. Seventy-eight Nols, numbered 1813–1890, were built, finally disappearing in 1959. 1815 is seen at the new Gatwick Airport in 1958. (*J. H. Aston*)

For the Portsmouth No. 1 and No. 2 electrifications, four-car, rather than six-car, units were used. These were gangwayed to allow all passengers to reach restaurant or buffet facilities, giving the units a 'one-eyed' look, hence the nickname 'Nelsons'. 4 Cor units 3101–3129 were for the Portsmouth No. 1 scheme, along with the 4 Res (restaurant) units, 3054–3072. Cors 3130–3155 and 4 Buf (buffet) units 3073–3085 were for the No. 2 scheme, which operated from Victoria along the mid-Sussex route via Horsham and Arundel. All units were in service by July 1938 and lasted until October 1972. 4 Cor 3111 waits at London Bridge with a Littlehampton train in April 1949. (*J. H. Aston*)

4 Buf unit 3083 heads a peak-hour Littlehampton train through Purley in the early 1970s. (*SEG Archive*)

One complete 4 Cor unit, 3142, plus a Driving Motor Brake Second Open (DMBSO) from unit 3135, have been preserved by the Southern Electric Group. Most of these vehicles are now on the East Kent Railway at Shepherdswell, Kent, giving visitors a chance to experience travel in a 1930s, Maunsell-era EMU. The interior of DMBSO 11187 is pictured on 14 July 2013. (*Simon Jeffs*)

An experimental six-car trailer unit, 6 TC No. 601, was made-up in June 1965 from de-motored Cor motor coaches and four Pul/Pan trailers. It entered service in January 1966 hauled by an adapted Class 33 loco on Oxted Line services, later transferring to the Clapham Junction–Kensington Olympia shuttle. It was intended to be the prototype for a push-pull Oxted Line fleet, but no further examples were converted and 601 was taken out of use in June 1971. (*SEG Archives*)

The successor to the 4 Sub units was the Southern-designed 4 EPB fleet (later, Class 415). Although a direct descendant of the Subs, a number of technological advances were incorporated, the major change being the fitting of the electro-pneumatic (EP) brake in addition to a Westinghouse brake – hence, EPB. Unit 5256, with an 'S' prefix, enters Norwood Junction in 1957. (*A. J. Wills collection © Southernrailway.net*)

The next set of EPBs were a batch of two-car units (5651–5684; later, Class 416) on reclaimed 2 Nol underframes. From the early 1980's, these were at Selhurst and often used on 'Cat/Tat' (Caterham and Tattenham Corner) services, a stronghold of the EPBs. 5670 is seen at Purley on a Caterham train. (*Bryan Rayner*)

The interior of preserved 2 EPB unit 5759, as preserved on the East Kent Railway in March 2013. The 2H/3H DEMUs had an almost identical layout. (*Brendan Gash*)

The first post-war development of express EMU stock were the Ceps. These were an almost direct descendant of the Cors, but with an EP braking system and electrical controls similar to the EPB units and, like the contemporary BR Mark 1 coach, incorporated more modern materials (formica and aluminium, rather than wood and brass). Six prototypes (4 Cep 7101–4, 4 Bep (with buffet car) 7001–2) were sent to Brighton in 1956/7, but fleet production was primarily for the Kent Coast electrification. They did, however, monopolise the Mid-Sussex workings after withdrawal of the 4 Cor/Buf units from this route in 1970. Prototype unit 7103 has just arrived at Earlswood on a trial run in July 1957. (*Arthur Tayler*)

THIRD RAIL EMUs, BRITISH RAILWAYS/ BRITISH RAIL 1965–1993

The 4 Bep units were rarely photographed, but here is 7007 in BR Blue-and-Grey livery, also passing Earlswood on an up Victoria service on 7 April 1979. (*John Atkinson*)

To replace the obsolete Pul/Pan express stock, a further new type of Mk 1 coach-derived EMU was designed in 1963. The new units were designated 4 Cig/ Big, 'IG' being the LBSCR telegraphic code for Brighton, but also stood for 'intermediate guard', indicating its position in the units. The BR Design Panel influenced the design and the interior accommodation and exterior appearance was much improved compared to the Ceps. Indeed, the units were renowned for their comfortable seating and good ride, a rarity on a Southern EMU! The first batch (Phase 1 units 7301–36; 4 Cig and 7031–48; 4 Big) emerged from York in 1964/5. The first of the Cig fleet, 7301, approaches Hassocks on a June evening in 1967. (*Michael Baker*)

Initially, the fleet was the last to be outshopped in a pleasing lined green livery. Later, they gained the ubiquitous BR blue-and-grey and were reclassified as Class 421 (Cigs) or 422 (Bigs). 7335 heads an Eastbourne service into East Croydon in May 1972. Additional Phase 2 units 7337–7438 and 7049–58 were introduced between 1970–2, displacing the Cor/Buf fleet. (*Bryan Rayner*)

Like the Cep fleet, the units were refurbished between 1985–93. Phase 1 units were renumbered in the 17xx series and Phase 2 units in the 18xx series. 1803, in Connex livery, waits in Platform 2 at Brighton on 19 August 2003. (*Tony Rispoli*)

It is a feature of the Southern Electric that its units undergo numerous reformations, particularly near the end of their working lives. In 1997, eleven 4 Big units had their compartments opened out and the buffet car removed. The units, reclassified 3 Cop (Class 421/7) and renumbered 1401–11, were used on Coastway services from Brighton. 1404 is seen at Lovers Walk depot on 21 August 2003. (*Tony Rispoli*)

A last look at a Cig, 1860, now in Southern Livery. This was one of twelve units to gain this livery from 2004, but all had been withdrawn as the reign of the 'Slammers' came to an end in November 2005. This is Clapham Junction on 13 May 2004 (*Tony Rispoli*)

The Lavs, Bils and Hals were replaced by the 4 Veps (later, Class 423) from 1968. These had three + two bench seating in Second Class and a slam door to each seating bay. In many ways, they were like a Sub or EPB, but with less comfortable seats! 7730 enters East Croydon in 1969. (*A. J. Wills collection © Southernrailway.net*)

In 1978, twelve Veps (7788–99) were fitted with luggage racks and a given a special 'Airport' livery for the Gatwick Airport–Victoria run. Reclassified 4 Veg and renumbered 7910–12, they reverted to their Vep identity from mid-1983 following introduction of the new Gatwick Express stock. 7907 approaches Clapham Junction on a snowy 10 January 1982. (*Brian Morrison*)

Between 1988–90, the Veps were internally facelifted. This involved the fitting of fluorescent lights,the opening-up of the guard's area to provide two additional seating bays and renumbering in the 34xx series. In 1998–9, Connex modified nineteen units in a similar fashion to the 3 Cops, opening out the compartments and abolishing First Class. Reclassified Class 423/9 (4 Vop), they were used on Metro services in South London. 3902 is seen at South Croydon, 22 September 2004. (*Brian Morrison*)

The interior of 4 Vop unit 3905. This unit is to be used by the 5Bel Trust to donate wheelsets for their 5 Bel restoration. Barrow Hill, Derbyshire, 30 March 2013. (*Simon Jeffs*)

Last days of the 'Slammers'. Class 423 unit 3514 has arrived at Victoria on the penultimate day of scheduled slam-door stock on the Brighton line, 18 August 2005. A few units continued to operate on an ad hoc basis until the very final day, 26 November 2005. (*Simon Jeffs*)

Examples of both SR and BR – design 2 Haps were transferred to the Coastway lines to replace the 4 Cors in 1971/2. In 1982, they were permanently formed into fixed four-car formations and reclassified 4 Cap. Units from the SR 1951 Haps were renumbered in the 32xx series and those from the BR 1957 batch into the 33xx series. They frequently escaped on trips to London and unit 3208 is seen here at East Croydon on 21 April 1983. On the left is a refurbished SR design Class 416/1 2 EPB unit, renumbered 6301. (*John Atkinson*)

Returning to the London suburbs, the PEP-derived Class 508 units were not found suitable for the duties required of them and a new, all-steel unit based on the Mark III coach body was designed specifically for Southern Region use. Designated Class 455, forty-six of these four-car, all Standard Class units, were allocated to Selhurst from 1984, allowing the last 4 Subs to be withdrawn. The first unit into service was (45) 5805, posing for its official photograph in 1983. (*SEG Archives*)

The livery variations of the Class 455s tell the history of the Southern Electric since 1983. Unit 5817 is seen at Norbury on 10 May 2004, still in Network Southeast livery. (*Tony Rispoli*)

While this remarkable photo shows a Class 455 in Connex livery at the rear of this ECS working at East Croydon, with another unit in Southern livery at the front, sandwiching a two-car Class 456 unit in NSE livery in the centre. 7 October 2004. (*Peter de Russet*)

Southern's Class 455 units were extensively refurbished from 2004. The front gangway was plated over, as evidenced in this view of unit 455829 at Clapham Junction on 10 December 2012. (*Simon Jeffs*)

The refurbished interior. From 2012, these units are being further refreshed. (*SEG Archives*)

To provide additional capacity and to replace the life-expired Class 416 units, a two-car derivative of the 455s, the Class 456, was introduced in 1990–91. Twenty-four units were built and actually had a toilet! Only one received Connex livery and was named *Sir Cosmo Bonsor*, after a chairman of the South Eastern Railway. Here he is at Clapham Junction on 19 May 2004. (*Tony Rispoli*)

The units received a less-extensive refurb between 2005-7 than the 455s, but the toilet was removed. All units were painted in Southern green, a livery they are not destined to wear for long as the whole fleet is to transfer to South West Trains in 2014 to work with their Class 455s. Two units, headed by 456013, enter Forest Hill on the 13 October 2012. (*Simon Jeffs*)

(Left) The light and airy interior of refurbished unit 456016 (*Lester Hayes*); (Right) Contrast with the low-backed seating in the unrefurbished 455 units. This is 5805, as delivered. (*SEG Archives*)

The first batch of sixty 4-car Class 319/0 units (319001–060) were built 1987/8 for the Bedford–Brighton Thameslink service, a flagship project by Network Southeast that commenced in May 1988. A further twenty-six Class 319/1 units were provided in 1990 (319161–186). These contained First Class accommodation and were diagrammed for Brighton line services. Both fleets were capable of 100mph operation and were dual voltage (25 kV AC OHLE; 750V DC third rail). Units 319009 *Coquelles* and 319008 *Cheriton* are seen at London Bridge prior to a record-breaking run to Brighton on 26 March 1994 in 37 minutes 57 seconds. (*Brian Morrison*)

Several livery variations have been used on Thameslink Class 319 units. This one was referred to as 'Cityscape', but was popularly known as the 'graffiti' livery! 319041 passes the former Pullman works at Preston Park on 29 October 1997. (*Chris Wilson*)

On privatisation, the Class 319 fleet was split, with 319001–20 going to the South Central franchise, awarded to Connex, with the rest remaining with Thameslink. Connex tasked Wolverton Traincare to convert seven of the units to a low-density Class 319/2 subgroup, with disabled toilet and 'snug' buffet area. These were used on the Connex (later, Brighton) Express service between Victoria and Brighton between January 1997 and May 2002. 319215 passes South Croydon in the summer of 1998. (*Colin Scott-Morton*)

The remaining thirteen units were not converted, but operated outer suburban services. Now (September 2013), Thameslink have them all back. A London Bridge–Horsham service is seen at East Croydon on 9 October 2006. (*Robert Armstrong*)

The Thameslink franchise was awarded to Govia, who promptly refurbished their fleet at Wolverton between 1997–8. The 319/0 fleet emerged as subclass 319/4, with new interiors, including First Class, and a blue with yellow and white stripe livery. In contrast, the 319/1s lost their First Class accommodation and were rebranded as the Standard Class-only Class 319/3. 319421 is seen at Salfords on a Bedford service, 13 August 2005. (*Arthur Tayler*)

The Thameslink franchise was transferred to First Group from April 2006, now marketed as First Capital Connect (FCC). FCC refreshed the units again, using vinyl wraps to apply a version of their purple/blue 'dynamic lines' livery. Many interior and mechanical modifications were also applied. 319456 units is seen at Brighton on 19 September 2012. (*Simon Jeffs*)

Is this the craziest livery ever seen on the Brighton line? Thameslink has been a phenomenal success and is being linked to the former Great Northern routes out of Kings Cross to Peterborough, Cambridge and Kings Lynn and into Kent. Additional capacity is being created in South London, with extra tracks between London Bridge and Blackfriars, and both stations being extensively rebuilt. To keep customers informed, a multi-striped format was used on all digital and paper literature and even found its way onto two Class 319/3 units! 319364, one of the pair, is seen at Blackfriars in April 2009. (*Kim Rennie*)

1,140 vehicles have been ordered from Siemens for the expanded Thameslink network to replace the Class 319 and 377/5 units currently in use. Fifty-five trains will run in twelve-car formations (Class 700/0) and sixty in eight-car formations (Class 700/1), with the first units expected in 2016. The image above depicts the initial livery, as agreed between the Department for Transport and FCC. (*Siemens*)

Connex South Eastern obtained a batch of twelve Class 508 units from Merseyside in 1996, and after refurbishment and reclassification as Class 508/2, used them on London Bridge to Tonbridge/Maidstone West and Maidstone West to Three Bridges services, both via Redhill. The Tonbridge services transferred to Southern in 2008 while the Three Bridges service was withdrawn from September 2006. All the Class 508/2s are now being scrapped. A rather tatty 508208 is seen at Coulsdon South with a train to Maidstone West on 23 August 2003. (*Tony Rispoli*)

The other PEP-derived units on the Brighton are the 1976-vintage Class 313/2 units, nineteen of which have operated Coastway services from Brighton for Southern since May 2010. The deployment of these units has been controversial, as although refurbished to a very high standard (below), they replaced the air-conditioned Class 377/3 units (with lavatories and First Class accommodation) on these routes. 313216 is seen at Brighton, 19 September 2012. (*Simon Jeffs*)

THIRD RAIL EMUs, PRIVATISATION TO PRESENT 1994–2013

The 'Electrostar/Turbostar' platform was developed by ADtranz (now Bombardier) in the late 1990s and is now the most numerous type of multiple unit found in the UK. Initially ordered by Connex for both its South Central and South Eastern franchises as replacements for their slam-door fleets, the first examples on the Brighton line did not arrive until 2001 and were subsequently delivered in Southern green livery. These comprised a fleet of twenty-eight three-car Class units, initially classified 375 (as in the above photo), becoming Class 377/3 on replacement of their Tightlock couplings with Dellners. (*SEG Archives*)

Next, from 2002, were sixty-four, four-car Class 377/1 units. The Standard Class arrangements require a bit of number-watching to get the best seats. The first twenty (377101-120) have 2+2 seating throughout (sit anywhere), 377121–139 have a mix of 2+2 and 3+2 in each coach, and 377140–164 have 2+2 in the Driving cars but 3+2 in the trailers (sit in coaches 1 and 4)! The doyen of the class, 377101, is seen at Gatwick Airport on 2 February 2013. (*Simon Jeffs*)

The interiors of class 377/1 units showing two+two seating in Connex (left) and Southern (right) layouts. (*'GB'*)

Fifteen Class 377/2 dual-voltage (25kV AC OHLE/750V DC third rail) units work services between South Croydon and Milton Keynes. 377208 is seen at Selhurst, 26 July 2012. (*Simon Jeffs*)

The 377/4 is the most numerous subfleet, sharing the same internal layout as 377140–164 and the 377/2 and 377/5 variants. Seventy-five units were bought into service to 2006. An example is seen on the London Road viaduct, Brighton, in 2006. (*Michael Baker*)

Twenty-three additional Class 377/5 units were ordered by Southern in 2008/9 and sub-leased to FCC for Thameslink services. Units 377521/507 approach Brighton on 13 April 2010. (*Chris Wilson*)

An extra twenty-six five-car Class 377/6 units are now entering service with Southern (September 2013) to provide additional capacity on the Metro routes. Eight additional dual-voltage units (377/7) are also on order to strengthen the Croydon–Milton Keynes service. 377604/6 are undergoing commissioning at Stewarts Lane Depot, 9 September 2013. (*Simon Jeffs*)

Interior seating is in 2+2 format throughout, all Standard Class. Note the extra handholds on the seats and the priority seats, 9 September 2013. (*Simon Jeffs*)

A derivative of the Electrostar platform, the Class 378 Capitalstar unit, was ordered by Transport for London (TfL) to operate its London Overground services, including those from West Croydon/Crystal Palace/New Cross to Highbury and Islington, and Clapham Junction–Stratford. These four-car units are air-conditioned with transverse seating along the bodysides and wide inter-car gangways, resembling TfL's Underground stock. Fifty-seven units, twenty third rail only (378135–154) and thirty-seven dual voltage (378201–234/255–257) entered service from 2010 and are currently being lengthened to five-car units. 378145 arrives at New Cross Gate. (*Simon Jeffs*)

Let us finish our survey of the passenger EMUs with a look at the two classes that have operated the Gatwick Express services since 2000. When National Express won the Gatwick Express franchise in April 1996, it was obligated to replace the ageing Mk II + Electro-Diesel rakes with new stock. An order was placed with Alstom for eight 8-car units (Class 460 – 8 Gat) which were delivered from 1999. The futuristic design earned them the nickname of 'Darth Vaders', after the *Star Wars* character. Two sliding doors/car gave access to a spacious interior layout with plenty of luggage space. 460004 passes Redhill on 5 November 2010. (*Peter Jones*)

During their time on the GATEX, many of the units were vinyled to advertise airlines operating from Gatwick. 460005 approaches East Croydon on 13 May 2004, bearing a Continental Airways livery. (*Brian Morrison*)

The classic view up Grosvenor Bank, Victoria. From left to right, Southeastern 375606, Southern's 377206, Gatwick Express 460002 and Southern's 377160. Two rakes of slam-door stock await the evening rush in Grosvenor Bank car sheds, while two Networker Class 465 units are parked outside. 460002 is on the 13:15 GATEX service to the airport and was one of the final two units in service during August 2012. The 460s have been transferred to SWT and will be converted to five-car Class 458/5 units, losing their distinctive nose cone in the process. 9 May 2005. (*Brian Morrison*)

Standard (left) and First Class (right) interiors of a Class 460 unit. (*'GB'*)

On introduction in 1988, the twenty-four five-car Class 442 units (5 Wes) could justifiably be described as Network Southeast's flagship EMU and retain a cult following among Southern Electric enthusiasts. Intended for long-distance travel between Waterloo and Weymouth, they were based on the Mark III bodyshell and were the last EMUs to be built with compartments for First Class passengers. In 2007, SWT withdrew the fleet and replaced them with Class 444 'Desiro' EMUs. Seventeen were transferred to Southern and entered service on an expanded Gatwick Express service from December 2008. To fit them for their new airport/commuting role, their interiors were extensively refurbished at Wolverton. The buffet car was removed, the compartments removed and First Class accommodation relocated to the centre of the train, to form a Motor Luggage Composite car. The remaining units transferred to Southern from 2009, and have been rebranded 'Express' to reflect their multiple roles. A 442 unit passes Salfords, 2 February 2013. (*Simon Jeffs*)

442414 waits under the inter-terminal transit South Terminal terminus at Gatwick Airport on 19 September 2012. The 'Express' branding is clearly visible. (*Simon Jeffs*)

The interior of a refurbished 442 unit – Standard Class (left) and First Class (right). Comfortable and quiet, these units have the best ambience of any EMU on the Brighton Line, although their lack of luggage space and single doors at the end of each coach do not allow fast entry and exit of passengers, particularly at Gatwick Airport. A refurbished five-car unit provides 322 Standard/twenty-four First Class seats, as opposed to 266/50 in an unrefurbished unit. (*Courtesy of Southern*)

The motorman watches the road
ahead in a 6 Pul unit in the 1930s...

... while his counterpart in a Class 319 cab remains just as vigilant. (*Paul Edwards Collection*)

DIESEL AND DIESEL-ELECTRIC MULTIPLE UNITS

The uniquely 'Southern' DEMU. 3H (Later Class 205) Unit 1101 heads towards South Croydon with an East Grinstead train on 20 October 1978. (*John Atkinson*)

The 3D, or 'Oxted' units, 1301–19, entered service on the lines linking London with Oxted, East Grinstead, Tunbridge Wells, Brighton (via Uckfield) and Eastbourne (via Heathfield), plus the Three Bridges to Tunbridge Wells line from April 1962. Unit 1317 is seen at Purley in July 1972, probably on an ECS working to St Leonards. (*Bryan Rayner*)

The unique, hybrid 'Tadpole' Class 3R DEMUs monopolised the Tonbridge–Reading trains until May 1979, when Western Region DMUs began to appear. 1206 is seen, in InterCity blue-and-grey, at Redhill on 22 May 1981, with the two DEMU vehicles at the front and the EMU one at the rear. (*Alex Dasi-Sutton*)

The 3R's replacements were the Class 119 Cross Country DMUs. Certain workings from Reading were extended to Gatwick Airport, from where this example has come. This picture was taken at Earlswood, 17 March 1981. (*Alex Dasi-Sutton*)

The Class 119 units were replaced by 'Networker Turbos', a DMU fleet introduced by Network Southeast for Chiltern Line and Thames Valley services. On privatisation, the Gatwick Airport–Redhill–Reading trains were operated initially by Thames Trains and, from April 2006, First Great Western (FGW). FGW use a mix of three-car air-conditioned Class 166 and non-air-conditioned Class 165 on these trains and an example of the latter, 165110, is seen at Redhill on 19 September 2012. (*Simon Jeffs*)

Two-car Class 171/7 Turbostar units are used on Southern's Brighton–Ashford service, with declassified First Class accommodation. However, although suitable for the Hastings–Ashford leg, they can become extremely overcrowded between Brighton and Hastings. 171721 is seen at Brighton, 2 February 2013. (*Simon Jeffs*)

Just off the Brighton line proper, a four-car Class 171/8 unit is seen at Crowborough with a London Bridge–Uckfield service on 1 November 2005. (*Arthur Tayler*)

The last Cross-Country service, formed of Class 220 Voyager unit 220021, waits to depart from Brighton with the 14:22 service to Birmingham New Street on 13 December 2008. With extension of the Thameslink system to Peterbrough and Cambridge from 2018, and Southern's Croydon to Milton Keynes service, many locations in the North, Midlands and East Anglia will be reached with one change. Perhaps there will be no further need for a 'Sunny South Express' in the future? (*'GB'*)

MISCELLANEOUS

To keep the third rail free of ice, a fleet of de-icing vehicles were converted from 1925-built motor coaches between 1959–60. Numbered 92–101 (later, 011–020), they were fitted with tanks for the de-icing fluid which was applied with special shoes to the conductor rail. However, what unit 018 was doing at Purley in June 1971 was anyone's guess! (*Bryan Rayner*)

The de-icing units have since been replaced by Multi-Purpose Vehicles which, as their name suggests, can be used for both leaf-clearing and de-icing duties. One is seen at Edenbridge in May 2006. (*Arthur Tayler*)

For a short period in 2009, Southern loaned eight of its 377/2s to FCC to cover stock shortages caused by the late delivery of 377/5 units and dual voltage Class 350/1 units, owned by London Midland, were transferred to Selhurst as replacements to operate the East Croydon–Milton Keynes service. 350 114 is seen at East Croydon. (*Lester Hayes*)

PRESERVED BRIGHTON LINE TRACTION

STEAM

Eighty-six 'Southern' steam locomotives (see www.semgonline.com/proto/pres-locos.html for the list) have been preserved. The most numerous LBSCR examples are the ten A1 and A1X Class 0-6-0T Terriers, with two on the Bluebell Railway, two on the Kent and East Sussex Railway and two on the Isle of Wight Railway. E1 Class 0-6-0T 110 is currently at the Isle of Wight Steam Railway, while E4 Class 0-6-2T 473 is on the Bluebell. B1 Class 0-4-2T *Gladstone* is at the National Railway Museum (NRM). One example of the N Class 2-6-0 moguls, 31874, lives at the Mid-Hants Railway, but four U Class moguls survive, two each at the Mid-Hants and Bluebell. One *King Arthur*, 777, is part of the National Collection. Bulleid Pacifics are numerous, with twenty located around the country, including on the Bluebell, Mid Hants and Swanage Railways. Several are certified for main-line use. Three of Maunsell's Schools Class 4-4-0s survive, plus single examples of the Q and Q1 0-6-0 freight engines. Finally, a reproduction Marsh Atlantic 4-4-2 is being built on the Bluebell Railway.

NON-STEAM LOCOS

Unfortunately, none of the 'Boosters' escaped the cutter's torch, but a single Class 71 Bo-Bo electric loco is in the care of the NRM. Many Class 03, 04, 08 and 09 diesel shunters are scattered around the country, as are examples of main-line diesel Classes 24, 25, 27, 31, 37, 42, 45, 47 and 52, all of which regularly visited the Brighton line on passenger, freight and excursion traffic. One of Bulleid's Class 12 shunters, 15224, is on the Spa Valley Railway. Many examples of the unique Class 33 'Cromptons' were saved, and even more Class 73 Electro-Diesels. Indeed, many of the latter, plus several Class 31, 37 and 47 locos still operate on the mainline. Opportunities to travel behind Class 33 and 73-hauled trains are provided by the Spa Valley Railway (www.spavalleyrailway.co.uk) and Swanage Railway (www.swanagerailway.co.uk). Diesel galas are held by many heritage railways – see the enthusiast press for details.

Terrier tank No. 8, *Freshwater,* is currently on the Isle of Wight Railway. It is seen here on 21 August 2013. (*Colin Duff*)

Over on the Mid-Hants, visitors can travel behind N Class 2-6-0 loco 1874...

... or Schools Class 4-4-0 *Cheltenham*. Both are seen on 22 September 2012. (*Simon Jeffs*)

Several West Country Class 4-6-2 locomotives have been passed for main-line operation. Here is 34067, *Tangmere,* at Eastbourne on 27 January 2007. (*Simon Jeffs*)

EMUs AND DEMUs

A comprehensive list of preserved EMUs and DEMUs is provided by the Southern Electric Group at *www.southernelectric.org.uk/preservation/preserved-stock/index.html*. Space precludes a description of all these units, but notable examples which can be viewed and travelled in include:-

- 14 of the 15 ex 5 Bel Cars. Three are currently formed in the VSOE British Pullman train while six are at Barrow Hill, being restored to a main-line certified Bel unit. For more details, see *www.brightonbelle.com* and *www.orient-express.com*
- 4 Cor unit 3142, in the care of the Southern Electric Group. Currently, two vehicles operate as a 2 Cor unit at the East Kent Railway. See *www.southernelectric.org.uk*
- 2 Bil unit 2090, currently at the NRM's outstation at Shildon. See *www.nrm.org.uk*
- 2 EPB unit 5759 and 4 Cep unit 7105, in the care of the EPB Preservation Group. See *www.epbpg.co.uk* and *www.eastkentrailways.co.uk* for operating days
- 4 Sub 4732, 2 Hap 4311 and 2 EPBs 6307 and 5793 can be viewed at Open Days at the Electric Railway Museum Coventry. See *www.electricrailwaymuseum.co.uk*
- 3 Cig units 1497 and 1498 operate occasionally on the Mid-Norfolk (*www.mnr.org.uk*) and Epping-Ongar Railways (*http://eorailway.co.uk*)
- Relive the 1984-2002 Gatwick Express by travelling in ex-GATEX Mk II coaches on the Ecclesbourne Valley Railway (*www.e-v-r.com*)
- One should also not forget 4 Vep unit 3417 *Gordon Pettit*. Owned by the Bluebell Railway, Gordon is much in demand for Gala events at many Southern heritage lines

Turning to DEMUs, Hasting Diesels Ltd maintains a fleet of DEMU vehicles which often run as unit '1001', which is certified for main-line operation. See www.hastingsdiesels.co.uk for rail tours. Working Class 205 and 207 DEMUs are operated by many heritage railways, including the Spa Valley Railway, Lavender Line (*www.lavender-line.co.uk*), Mid-Hants Railway (*www.watercressline.co.uk*), Epping-Ongar railway and Eden Valley Railway (*www.evr.org.uk*).

The sole mainline Southern electric loco preserved is Class 71 E5001. It operated in top-and-tail mode with 33108 and 4 Vop 3905 at the Barrow Hill Depot 'Southern Saturday' event on 30 March 2013 but was not operational. (*Simon Jeffs*)

Also on show at the Southern Saturday event were five ex-5 Bel cars which are being restored to a working 5 Bel unit by the 5 Bel Trust. As this may comprise cars from all three 5 Bel units, it has gained the new number 3050 (or should that be 403 001?). (*Simon Jeffs*)

Two young enthusiasts look forward to a ride on Class 33 Crompton 33065/6585 *Sealion* on the Spa Valley Railway on 5 May 2007. (*Simon Jeffs*)

Turning to EMUs and, by a remarkable coincidence, 4 Cor unit 3142 and 4 Vep unit 7717 (later 3417), which have both been preserved, are seen side-by-side in BR service at Waterloo in 1970. (*Clinton Shaw*)

DMBSOs 11161 and 11187 form a 2 Cor unit that operated on the East Kent Railway on 14 July 2013, the first time the Southern Electric Group's Cor has operated as a multiple unit since the 1980s. (*Chris Reavell*)

'Gordon' goes to the seaside! 4 Vep unit 3417, top-and-tailed by Class 33 loco 6515 and Class 73 electro-diesel 73136, pass Corfe Castle on the Swanage Valley Railway on 23 May 2007. (*Mark Pike*)

Back at the East Kent Railway (EKR), the EPB Preservation Group's (EPBPG) 4 Cep 7105 celebrates its 50th birthday at Shepherdswell on 21 September 2008. (*'GB'*)

Suburban EMUs can also be sampled on the EKR. The EPBPG's 2 EPB unit 5759 has been beautifully restored to late 1960's Southern Region green livery in this image taken on 19 August 2006. The EKR is not electrified, EMUs being pushed and pulled by a Class 09 shunter! (*Simon Jeffs*)

The National Railway Museum's 2 Bil unit, 2090, was a favourite for railtours in the 1980s, often running with 4 Sub 4732. 2090 is seen here at Pevensey and Westham on the 'Electric Phoenix' railtour on 23 September 1984. Unfortunately, preserved EMUs are currently barred from operating on Network Rail metals. (*Adrian Willats*)

DEMUs are understandably popular with heritage railways, and the English Electric 4SRKT engine does make a wonderfully-nostalgic growl! Here, the DMBSO from unit 1133 is seen on the Lavender Line on 8 July 2012. (*Simon Jeffs*)

BIBLIOGRAPHY

Bradley, D. L., *Locomotives of the LBSCR* (3 Volumes). (RCTS, 1969/1972/1974).

Brown, D., 'Development of the London Suburban Network and its Trains' *Southern Electric: A New History*. Volume 1 (St Leonards on Sea: Capital Transport Publishing, 2009).

Brown, D., 'Main Line Electrification, the War Years and British Railways' *Southern Electric: A New History*. Volume 2. (St Leonards on Sea: Capital Transport Publishing, 2010).

Bonavia, M. R., *The History of the Southern Railway* (London; Unwin Hyman, 1987).

Cooper, B. K., *Rail Centres: Brighton*. (Birmingham: Ian Allan, 1981).

Cross, D., *The Larger Brighton Locomotives*. (Birmingham: Ian Allan, 1984).

Elsey, L., *Profile of the Southern Moguls*. (Oxford Publishing Co., 1986).

Faulkner, J.N., *Rail Centres: Clapham Junction*. (Birmingham: Ian Allan, 1991).

Grant, S., *The LBSCR Elevated Electrification: A Pictorial View of Construction*. (Southampton: Noodle Books, 2011).

Grant, S. & Jeffs, S., *The Brighton Belle – The Story of a Famous and Much-Loved Train*. (St Leonards on Sea: Capital Transport Publishing, 2012).

Gray, A., *The London to Brighton Line 1841-1977*. (Usk: The Oakwood Press 1977).

Haresnape, B. & Swain, A., *British Rail Fleet Survey 10: third rail DC Electric Multiple Units* (Birmingham: Ian Allan, 1989).

Haresnape, B., *Bulleid Locomotives* (Birmingham: Ian Allan, 1985).

Jeffs, S., *London to Brighton Through Time* (Stroud: Amberley Publishing, 2013).

Linecar, H.W.A., *British Electric Trains* (Birmingham: Ian Allan, 1947).

Marsden, C. J., *Southern Electric Multiple Units, 1898-1948* (Birmingham: Ian Allan, 1983).

Marsden, C. J., *Southern Electric Multiple Units, 1948-1983* (Birmingham: Ian Allan, 1983).

Marsden, C. J., *The Electro-Diesels: An Illustrated History of Classes 73 and 74* (Oxford Publishing Co., 2006).

Marshall, D., *History of the Southern Railway* (reprint). (Birmingham: Ian Allan, 1988).

Mitchell V. & Smith K., *Three Bridges to Brighton* (Eastbourne: Middleton Press, 1986).

Mitchell V. & Smith K., *Victoria to East Croydon* (Eastbourne: Middleton Press, 1987)

Mitchell V. & Smith K., *London Bridge to East Croydon* (Eastbourne: Middleton Press, 1988).

Mitchell V. & Smith K., *East Croydon to Three Bridges* (Eastbourne: Middleton Press, 1988).

Moody, G. T., *Southern Electric 1909-1979* (5th Edn.) (Birmingham: Ian Allan, 1979).

Morrison, B. & Vaughan, J., *The Power of the 33s* (Oxford Publishing Co., 1982).

Nock, O. S., *Southern Steam* (London: Pan Books Ltd., 1972)

Nock, O. S., *British Locomotives of the 20th Century* Volume 1. (PSL 1983).

Nock, O. S., *British Locomotives of the 20th Century* Volume 2. (PSL 1984).

Pallant, N. & Bird, D., *BR Locomotives: 1. Diesel and Electric Locomotives of the Southern Region*. (Birmingham: Ian Allan, 1984).

Rayner, B., *Southern Electrics: A Pictorial Survey*. (Truro: D. Bradford Barton Ltd. 1975).

Rayner, B and Brown, D., *The 4 SUB Story*. (Southern Electric Group 1983).

Robertson, K. 2009. *The Leader Project. Fiasco or Triumph?* (Oxford Publishing Co.)

Scott-Morgan, J., *Maunsell Locomotives*. (Birmingham: Ian Allan, 2002).

Tayler, A., *A Lifetime in Traction. An Engineer on the Southern Diesels and Electrics*. (Southampton: KRB Publications, 2004).

Townroe, S. C., *Arthurs, Nelsons and Schools of the Southern* (Birmingham: Ian Allan, 1973).

Welch, M. *Southern DEMUs* (St Leonards on Sea: Capital Transport Publishing, 2004).

ACKNOWLEDGMENTS

First, I must thank Louis Archard at Amberley Publishing for allowing me to complete my survey of the Brighton Line. Second, thanks again to the numerous photographers, archivists, curators and publishers who have provided images for both this and the previous volume 'London to Brighton through Time'. Space precludes including those whom I acknowledged previously, but I wish to add to the role of honour - Mike Esau, Brian Jackson, Clinton Shaw, Adrian Willats, Bryan Rayner, Colin Duff, Brendan Gash, John Atkinson, Peter de Russet, Robert Armstrong, Ashley Saunders, Chris Reavell, Mark Pike, Kim Rennie and 'GB'. Mike Turner provided the wonderful painting of Brighton Station in the 1960s. Paul Edwards' website on the Brighton motive power depots, http://thebrightonmotivepowerdepots.yolasite.com provided many more images and sources while Chris Pancutt, Yvonne Leslie and Gerry McFadden at Southern facilitated photography of EMUs at locations on the Southern Network. Laurie Mack, Stephen Grant, John Minnis and Tony Hillman proof-read the text, so any errors remaining are my own. Finally, thanks to my wife Laurel who has reconciled herself to the fact that Railway Disease is incurable; my father, Stanley Jeffs, whom I now take out train-watching, in return for the times he took me, and my late brother, Tim Jeffs (BR (SR) and SWT driver), who keeps an eye on me from the great railway depot in the sky.

Simon Jeffs, Eastbourne